How to Earn a Comfortable Living as a Freelance Writer

What It Takes to Set Up a Freelance Writing Business That Pays the Bills…And Then Some

How to Earn a Comfortable Living as a Freelance Writer

What It Takes to Set Up a Freelance Writing Business That Pays the Bills…And Then Some

Christina M. DeBusk

Copyright © 2017
All Rights Reserved

Other Books

by

Christina M. DeBusk

I've Always Wanted to Write a Book! 10 Easy-to-Follow Steps to Becoming a First Time Author

The 15 Minute Total Life Makeover: 12 Ways to Dramatically Change Any Area of Your Life in Just 15 Minutes a Day

Life Lessons: What I Learned During My Career in Law Enforcement...and in Life

Rock Solid A.B.B.s (Attitudes, Beliefs, and Behaviors) for Weight Loss Success

Pessimist to Positivist

Catching Happiness

AUTHOR'S NOTE

The scanning, uploading and distribution of this book via the internet or any other means without the permission of the publisher is illegal and punishable by law. Please purchase only authorized editions and do not participate in or encourage piracy of copyrighted materials. Your support of the author's rights is appreciated.

Table of Contents

Introduction 1
Ch 1. Know Your Why..11
2. Equipment & Supplies..17
3. Identify Your Niche..23
4. Learn the Craft..35
5. Develop Your Brand 47
6. How to Find Clients 57
7. Setting Your Rates & Fees 69
8. Getting Paid..79
9. Other Business Considerations...................................87
Now Write 97

Introduction

I've always envied people who have always known what they wanted to do for a living. People who, at a young age, declare to their parents, grandparents, and friends that they're going to be a fireman, a police officer, a lawyer, or a doctor when they grow up…and then become one.

I was never that person. Or, at least that's what I thought.

When I was little, I don't remember having any real career goals whatsoever. Probably my first recollection is when I was in middle school, when I decided that what I wanted more than anything was to become a psychologist.

This was primarily because I wanted to work directly with people who were struggling in their personal or professional lives. I wanted to help them become happier, to enjoy their worlds just a little bit more.

That is, until I got into college, took some classes, and discovered that I loved sociology *even more*. From that moment on, I decided that social work was actually my calling.

I knew I likely wouldn't make much money in that field, but I've never been money motivated, so that was okay. I just wanted to help people and who better to help than the underserved? And I was happy with my new career of choice, that is, until about two years before I graduated…

This is when I had to meet with my guidance counselor to make sure I'd have not only enough credits to obtain my diploma, but the right credits based on my sociology major, psychology minor (I guess I did stick with psychology in that regard), and social work concentration. Fortunately, I was in line with the right class schedule, but, since I had enough spare credits left over, she suggested that I also obtain a criminal justice concentration.

Sounds like fun, I thought. So that's what I did and, surprise, I fell in love with that subject too! So in love, in fact, that, after graduating, I spent the next 15 years working in law enforcement in one capacity or another.

Fresh out of college, I was hired to create a legal advocate position for a local domestic violence shelter. Then, one year later, I transitioned to working for the courts, first as a caseworker, then as an enforcement officer.

In this second role, which is the role I spent most of that portion of my career in, I transported prisoners, sought felony warrants, and testified in court. I also enforced court orders related to custody, parenting time, and child support that involved other states, sometimes other countries.

On weekends, for "fun," I spent time as a reserve deputy, which meant that I went out on the road in uniform with full time patrol officers and did the same job they did, I just had no powers of arrest unless I was with them and, oh yeah, I didn't get paid.

Well, that's not entirely true. I didn't get paid in money anyway. I was actually paid in the satisfaction of knowing that I was there to help people in my community, often in their darkest hours.

All in all, I enjoyed what I wound up doing for a living, I really did. That's why, when I was faced with the opportunity to move 2,500 miles from home (from Michigan to California), it really made my head spin.

Did I have enough energy to start over and reestablish myself with another law enforcement agency (something that is no easy feat, especially when your partner has to trust you with his or her life)…or was it time to do something different?

This was the point in my life when I realized that maybe I *had* been that person who always knew what she wanted to do, I just wasn't paying attention.

Looking back on my younger years, I remembered having this vision of me as a writer. In this image, I was always sitting with a hot cup of coffee (isn't that what all writers drink?) near a picture window with the beauty of nature beyond, typing out this great story that everyone would be just dying to read.

Though I was kind of excited about the idea, several doubts immediately set in. Was *now* the time to make that dream a reality? Did I have what it takes to be a full-time, professional writer? Could I even make a living doing the one and only thing I could ever remember myself wanting to do as a child?

After many months of running the pros and cons of taking this type of leap, I ultimately decided that that it was time for a change. Besides, if this was the life I wanted, what better time to go and get it than when I'm moving and going to have to find a new job anyway?

So that's what I did. I hung up my handcuffs and traded it in for a computer with Microsoft Word. It was time to change the world with my words versus my hands.

Although I'd love to tell you that it has been rainbows and kittens ever since, that isn't exactly the case. In the spirit of "telling it like it is" so that you know what to expect should you decide to take the same journey, it didn't take me long to learn that the writing life wasn't what I had envisioned. At all.

Because I didn't have the money for a full sized desktop computer, my writing was going to have to be on one of those teeny, tiny netbooks. And that hot cup of coffee? Yeah, not quite. I was lucky if it was even lukewarm half the time.

I didn't even get that picture window of my dreams. Instead, I worked in the kitchen area of a small apartment, which meant that the only window I could look out was next to the fridge and actually overlooked the parking lot. So much for nature.

No, nothing was as I'd imagined. Instead, I spent 12, 14, and 16 hours a day in a little cubbyhole, leaning over a tiny netbook while learning everything I could about the craft of writing.

I studied all of the different publications I wanted to write for and researched the best way to reach out to them. I read book after book, article after article, and blog after blog, looking for tips and inspiration about how to be successful with this new craft. I took in as much information as my overworked brain could stand, and then I'd take in some more.

Fortunately, within the first few months, I hooked up with a successful marketer who was generous enough with his time to teach me what he know about content writing and how to create copy that sells. He shared with me which books would help me the most, even buying some and having them sent to me.

I soaked in as much information as I could from him while still looking for other clients. I knew I needed to write for several businesses if I was going to make this new career work.

At first, most of the jobs I took didn't even pay minimum wage. I took them anyway because I wanted to gain experience and grow my portfolio. Yes, I was working more hours than I ever had in my life (and making less than I ever had), but I accepted it as part of the learning process. I needed to "pay my dues."

Now here I sit, several years and more than 4,000 completed projects later, earning *more* than I did in my full-time law enforcement job, and happier than I ever thought I could be. Yet, looking back, I realize now that I took the hard way to becoming a freelance writer.

I say this because I didn't have someone telling me exactly what I needed to do to be successful as a freelance writer. Although I had the marketer who was extremely generous with his time, I didn't have another writer as a mentor. I didn't have someone who was in the exact career that I wanted who was saying, "Okay, do this" or "Now, do that."

Instead, I had to take what I learned from a bunch of different resources to develop my writing business. This took months and months of time and energy, both of which I could have saved had I had just one person who was willing to share everything I needed to know in my journey to becoming a freelance writer.

Though I went without that luxury, I don't want any other new freelance writer to be in that position. That's why I decided to write this book (and also why I now offer writing coaching). I want to share what knowledge I have with you so you can earn a comfortable living as a freelance writer. I want to be your coach *and* your cheerleader, guiding you and cheering you on as you work your way through this sometimes cutthroat career.

At this point, you may be wondering why I want you to just make a "comfortable" living when a lot of other books out there can teach you how to reach a six-figure income. Here's my response:

Not all freelance writers are in this for the money.

I'm not going to lie, I could definitely find some places to spend money if my revenue shot up to the 100k mark. But it's even more important to me to not have the jam packed schedule that often comes with making that kind of wage.

According to the Bureau of Labor Statistics, the 2016 median wage for writers and authors was $61,240 per year[i]. So, if I can be somewhere around that amount (which I am) and still have some time to enjoy life, I'm good.

I no longer want to be stuck behind a computer all day. I want to be a writer who also has a life, and, if that's how you feel too, then this is the book for you.

To be clear, this doesn't mean that I don't think you should aim big or try to earn as much as you can. If that's what you want, if that's what motivates you and will make your life complete, then, by all means, that's what you should do! But I also want you to do it with both eyes open.

What I mean by this is, I want you to understand that some salary websites put a freelance writer's median pay at $24.45 per hour[ii]. Multiply that by 40 hours a week and 50 weeks a year (you want at least two weeks off, right?)

and that comes out to $48,900 a year. Still other sites place it lower, or closer to $42k[iii].

Can you make more than this and defy the averages? Of course you can! I do and I know of several other freelance writers who make a very good living in this career.

Bob Bly (www.bly.com), author of *Secrets of a Freelance Writer: How to Make $100,000 a Year or More* and *Marketing Dictionary for the 21st Century*, is one that I've had the pleasure of interviewing for one of my articles for *Businessing Magazine*. Not only has he created a successful career as a freelance writer, if you go to his website, you'll see that he currently has 93 of his own books in print. This is only my seventh, so I can't imagine writing and publishing almost 100 books!

Another writer who is successful in this field is Carol Tice. In addition to authoring numerous writing-related guides and books, she also runs the Freelance Writers Den (https://freelancewritersden.com/). That's where I got to know her a little bit as I spent some time in one of her mastermind groups.

My point is, if a 6-figure income is what *you* are after, then those types of resources will probably satisfy you more. However, after studying the lives of and talking face-to-face with some highly successful freelancers, it's clear to me that they have only achieved those levels of income by putting in some super long days, so be ready for that too.

Again, if that's what you want to do and you're willing to put in the work to do it, that's great. The things you'll learn in this book can still help you achieve that goal.

I've just learned that, at this point in my life, that's not what *I* want. I used to think I did. Every year, I'd set a goal to make $100k plus no matter how many hours it took me to make it. Not anymore.

In honesty, had I kept going like I was, working 12-16 hour days six days a week, I don't even know if I'd still be writing. After a couple years of it, I noticed that I wasn't enjoying my work like I wanted. I was basically burning myself out.

Plus, once I was truly honest with myself, I also came to the realization that money isn't what motivates me. It's helping others reach *their* goals.

Whether it's the small business owner that I helped achieve first page Google ranking to grow his business or the woman that I helped get her ideas out by ghostwriting her book, I know that I'm leaving the world a better place.

This is why I am happy as a freelance writer. But what about you? Why do you want to be a freelance writer?

It's very important that you know this, which leads me to my next point…

Ch 1. Know Your Why

Any time that you're in business for yourself, whether it's working as a freelance writer or in some other field, there are going to be good days and bad.

The good days are the days you make progress. These are the days you get the big jobs and finally feel like your hard work is paying off. They're also the days when it feels like everything is going your way, almost effortlessly. The bad days are the complete opposite.

Those are the days where you walk to the mailbox, yet again, only to return without the check that *should* be there but your client consistently pays late. They are also the days that you send out 25 cold emails and receive not one reply.

I've had days where I've gone completely redone my website, only to realize that my branding is off. I've also had days where, no matter how much work I've done for clients (sometimes for free!), it just wasn't enough.

These are the days that will make you wonder why you're working day and night, sometimes writing straight through the weekends and not taking holidays off…what's it all for? When you have enough of these in a row, it may even cause you to question whether or not your dream of being a freelance writer is worth it.

There have been a couple of times in my writing career where I've decided to give it all up and interview for a job outside of the house. However, the last time I was at this point, between the interview itself and waiting to hear whether or not I got the job, I really began to think deeply about whether a career change was really what I wanted, or if I was just trying to take the easy way out.

That's when I forced myself to sit down and make a list of all of the reasons why freelance writing is so important to me. I wanted to know whether this was a career worth fighting for or if I was truly done.

By the time I finished, my list looked something like this:

- *I get to set my own hours.* No more asking for time off to handle all of life's other obligations, like doctors' appointments and dentist visits. Better yet, not more being denied the time because someone else was dictating my work hours. As a freelance writer, I can get my groceries in the middle of the day if I'd like. Plus, when I take my daily exercise breaks, I can do them whenever I want, not at a predesignated time.

- *I can do my work when I'm most productive.* This is *huge* for me because I often get up before 5 AM and start my work day then. This is when my mind is clear and I'm able to focus as, usually by the afternoon, I find it a struggle to write fluidly. Then there are the days where I don't feel productive at all. When those happen, I do other business stuff and take a day off from writing completely. I can do this because I'm self-employed.

- *I have greater control over my income.* No, I can't control who chooses to hire me and who doesn't, but I'm also not pigeon-holed into a job where I get a predetermined hourly wage for a set number of hours per week. If I want to make more money for an upcoming vacation or if I have higher bills the following month, I simply work more hours or charge more for projects. In the end, it's all up to me how much I make.

- *I get to pick who I work with.* One of the greatest pleasures of being self-employed is that, for the first time in my professional life, I actually get to pick who my clients are. This means that if it isn't really working well between a particular client and I, I can simply tell them that I don't think we're a good fit and let them go. This is a major plus for me after spending 15 years working in law enforcement positions which, as you can imagine, often put me face-to-face with people who were less than excited about working with me.

- *I can work from anywhere.* Since I live in California, yet all of my family is either back in Michigan or in the U.K., being able to work from many different locations is important to me.

Granted, I don't try to fill all of my family time with work projects, but I am typically an early riser, so I'm still able to make a couple of bucks on my vacations since I'm usually up before everyone else in the house. I also go back to Michigan every Packzi Day to help my aunt at her bakery. (Can you believe that we sell more than 12,000 of these jelly and cream-filled donuts in just one day, in a town that only has just over 1,000 people[iv]?) Being a freelance writer allows me to do this without having to take an entire week off of work.

- *I don't have a long commute.* Because my office is right down the hall, I've eliminated any commute time, which means that I have more time to handle my business. While this isn't a huge factor in Michigan, if you've ever been to California and been stuck in the traffic out here, then you know how much time this can potentially save!

- *No more dressing up.* When I worked at the courthouse, I had to wear dress clothes every day. On weekends, I wore a uniform. Now I spend my days in shorts and a t-shirt. I do have to admit that there are times that I do miss getting dressed up and going into work. However, I only miss it on occasion, definitely not enough to make it worth going back to it full-time.

These are just some of the reasons why making my freelance writing career work is so important to me. As such, these are also what keep me going when all I want to do is quit.

So, what is *your* why? Why is becoming a freelance writer so important to *you*?

I want you to take a few minutes right now and make a list of all of the reasons you want to have your own freelance writing business. Don't worry about whether your answers are right or wrong, good or bad. This is all about figuring out why this career choice is so important to *you*.

Once it's complete, take this list and stash it in your desk drawer. Pull it out every time you're ready to give up and walk away from your dream. Look it over and read each item—each reason—one by one to remind yourself of why you should keep moving forward, even if it's the last thing you feel like doing.

Okay. You've identified your reasons why to keep you motivated, so the next step is to make sure you have the right tools for the job. What are they?

Let's go into that now…

2. Equipment & Supplies

Every profession has its own set of equipment and supplies needed in order to "get the job done." Doctors need stethoscopes, construction workers need jack hammers, and carpenters need saws. So what do freelance writers need?

A Computer (or Two)

The days of the typewriter are gone (thankfully!) and, though some people still prefer to write with pen and paper, the reality is that you need a computer not only to create your content, but also to share it and correspond easily and quickly with clients. There's really no way around it.

If you generally work from one location—whether from a home office or an outside office or designated workspace—then a desktop would likely make the most sense. However, if like to write from coffee shops or prefer to work outdoors on the beach or next to a stream cascading down the mountainside, then you'll definitely need a laptop.

Personally, I have both because, while I generally work at my desk in my home office, if I'm traveling and still want to work, I need something I can easily take with me. But if you're strapped on cash and can only pick one, then just pick the one that makes the most sense for your writing lifestyle.

As far as brands are concerned, my desktop is an HP and my laptop is a Toshiba and I've been more than happy with both. One thing to note though is, if you do choose to get two computers, you want to make sure they have the same operating systems so you can switch back and forth with relative ease. It is super frustrating if they work differently and you have to stop and think before doing basic tasks.

I chose a pretty standard computer for both to help keep my costs down, which means that I opted for no major bells and whistles or high-priced software or programs that came pre-installed. Realistically, as long as I can search the internet and have access to Word, I'm good. This means that I was able to spend less than $1,000 on each, so I was happy about that.

The only thing that I did not compromise on was screen size. I have a 27 inch monitor for my desktop and love it because I can have the internet up on one side and my document on the other and I can see both just fine. This was a HUGE step up for me, considering I spent the first entire year of my writing career on that netbook! (Can you say neck pain?)

A Printer

The second thing you'll need as a full-time freelance writer is a good quality printer. Though most of my work is saved digitally, I still like to keep a paper copy of my work orders and receipts, so a printer is a must.

I just went printer shopping a year ago and the one I chose to buy was an HP Color Laser Jet Pro MFP M277dw. It cost me around $350 and each color cartridge (there are four) is somewhere around $70-80 apiece.

When I first started out, I had an inkjet. Though it worked okay, after switching to a toner printer, I will never go back. Granted, the cartridges are more expensive by about $30-40 each, but they also last a whole lot longer (like up to 2,500 copies each compared to just a few hundred), which means that I don't have to order them as often either.

Of course, the printer needs paper and, since most of the copies I make are just for me, I tend to stick to the cheap stuff. I also buy it a box at a time as opposed to by the ream, which cuts the cost even more.

If you plan to send any of your content out to clients, then you'll likely want to invest in higher quality paper than that. Remember that, the more professional your work looks, the more professional *you* look, so don't skimp.

If you're someone who is super organized, you could even buy colored paper and print different things on different colors. Maybe your business receipts will go on light yellow, your work projects on mint green, and your client notes on baby blue. Some may say that this is overkill, but I say that it's your business, so do whatever you'd like! Besides, you'll likely be the only one who sees most of your print-offs anyway, so what's the big deal?

Other Miscellaneous Supplies You'll Likely Want Up Front

Though a computer and printer are the two main tools that you'll use in your day-to-day grind as a freelance writer, there are other supplies that I use quite often and suggest that you buy early on. There may be other things you realize you need along the way, but these are the things I use almost every day as a writer:

- Sticky notes in a variety of sizes, for when you want to leave yourself little reminders
- Tabbed vanilla folders, one for each of your projects or clients
- Legal pads, for drafting book outlines or to take notes during client phone calls that occur when you're not in front of your computer
- Pens, pencils, and highlighters
- USB memory sticks to save your work
- A weekly planner to keep you on track so you don't miss a deadline
- Stapler and staples
- Paper clips

Once you have these basics, you're ready to delve into your new writing business a little more. But first, before you get too far ahead of yourself, you'll want to identify your niche.

3. Identify Your Niche

If you're like I was when I first started out, you may be saying, "*Um, okay. I can do that, but first, what's a niche?*"

A niche is basically a specific field or topic area. For instance, I write only for entrepreneurs and small business owners who want content related to health and wellness, personal development, small business ownership, and personal safety. These are the areas I know best and, therefore, the ones I can contribute the most effective content in.

There are many ways you can go with your niche but, before you pick one, you may want to ask yourself: What type of writer do I want to be?

If you're not entirely sure how to answer that, here are some questions that can help lead you in the right direction:

- Do you want to write fiction or non-fiction?
- Do you want to write for yourself, for clients, or both?
- When it comes to style of writing, are you more of a technical writer, academic writer, or conversational writer (which means that you write much like you speak)?
- What specific field or fields do you want to write about?

I know. It's a lot to try to figure out right up front. However, taking the time to really sit and think about what type of writer you want to be <u>before</u> you start your freelance writing business can save you a ton of time in the future. It can also help you understand how to better align your business so that you position yourself directly in front of your ideal customer.

When I first started out, I didn't take this approach. *You want me to write an article about something in the automotive industry? Well, I don't really know much on the topic, but I guess I can figure it out! A blog on custom yachts? Sounds fascinating. Sure, no problem.*

While it may seem like taking any type of job offered to you would give you a larger client base, providing access to more writing opportunities, it also hurts you because it keeps you from being seen as a specialist in certain fields. And if you've ever had to visit a specialist for medical reasons, you know that they not only do these doctors typically make more money, they're also more in demand.

This same principle carries over into the freelance world. The more expertise you have on a certain topic or with a specific type of writing, the more you can charge for your services. You're also more sought out because you become *the* expert that everyone wants to go to.

If you establish yourself well enough, you'll have clients coming from far and wide to work with you. In this case, they get the content they want and you get to earn a good wage, so everybody wins!

Once I realized this fact, I quit accepting any job that came my way and pared my services down to where, now, I only cover topics that I know and know well. Sure, sometimes I'll venture off and take something that isn't in one of my four fields, but only if I'm extremely interested in it and feel like I can do it without requiring a bunch of my time.

For instance, one of my clients recently asked me if I'd write some pieces in the financial niche. Certainly, I'm no accountant, but I do have a fair amount of knowledge when it comes to finances (in addition to managing my own retirement accounts, I spend 1-2 hours most days listening to finance-related podcasts), which means that I know enough of the lingo and basic principles to help give my client what he needs. In the end, I said yes and it's worked out well.

However, if you're just starting out, I would recommend that you stick with your niche topics. Don't worry so much about spreading out into other areas you're less familiar with until you've got some experience under your belt. Take it from me: You'll make yourself crazy if you do.

Types of Writing

Just as lawyers can specialize in civil or criminal law, and doctors can practice in any number of types of specialized medical fields (cardiology, rheumatology, dermatology), writers can specialize too. For instance, if you've ever searched job posts for writers, then you've likely seen a bunch of different types of writing jobs. But what does each one actually do?

Here are some of the most common:

- *Copywriter.* A copywriter focuses mainly on providing sales and marketing content for companies.

- *Content writer.* This type of writer helps businesses create content for their online and offline platforms to better engage their customer base.

- *Social media writer.* Social media writers create shareworthy content for companies to post on their social media sites.

- *Ghostwriter.* This writing job involves writing blogs, books, and other pieces of content for other people to publish in their name.

- *Book writer.* Just as it sounds, a book writer helps people write and publish their own books.

- *Technical writer.* Technical writers are responsible for creating manuals and guides for companies that develop various items, devices, and software.

- *Resume writer.* In this role, you'd spend your day writing and editing resumes to better connect job seekers with their dream employers.

- *Press release writer.* Any time a company releases a new product or service, they usually do a press release to get the media interested. In this role, you'd be responsible for helping companies write this announcement.

- *Grant writer.* Grant writers works for companies, oftentimes nonprofits, to help them secure funding for their programs.

- *Research writer.* Writers working in this capacity create content related to research, usually working in some type of academic setting.

- *Business plan writer.* A business plan writer helps business owners and operators formulate in-depth plans for how they want to run their company.

- *Proposal writer.* Some projects require companies to write proposals to be considered for the job, and this task is often hired out because the amount of money involved.

- *Playwright or screenwriter.* As the names suggest, a person in this role would spend their days writing plays or movies.

- *Song writer.* You can help singers create songs that touch the hearts of their listeners if you are a song writer.

- *Script writer.* This writer provides the scripts for a company to follow when creating their own videos or other forms of audio dialogue.

- *Poet.* A poet writes and publishes poems.

- *Comic writer.* This is a good writing job for someone who also likes to create their own graphics.

As you can see, many options exist when it comes to the type of writing you can do, and this list isn't even all inclusive. Basically, any time that words are being used, you can carve out a niche for yourself as a writer who provides that particular type of content.

To help you hone in on which one would work best for you personally, you want to think about three things: your areas of interest, your writing style, and where or how you'd like to be published. Let's look at each one now.

Areas of Interest

This may seem like common sense, but I'm surprised at how many aspiring writers I've worked with who have never thought of writing in a field that interests them as they are more concerned with where they can make the best money. Yet, the two are intertwined.

If you're not passionate about what you're writing about, if you don't have a decent level of interest in it, your content will fall flat. The reader will be able to see that you don't really care about the topic, which means that they won't want to read your work. And if you're working for someone else and their readership declines because of it, then you're not going to be working for them for long.

I remember when I first started out and I got a job for a company that wanted me to go through various types of stores and give a summarized version of what they sell, what their price point was, their shipping and return policies, and things like that. Ultimately, they wanted to be a website where shoppers around the world could go to learn more about an online business before deciding whether or not they'd order from them.

For this project, I wrote about e-commerce sites that sold everything from antiques to sporting equipment to clothing and other apparel. I remember one time, after turning in a set of stores, my editor emailed me back and said that it was apparent that I liked football from how I wrote that piece. That was my first lesson in the fact that how you feel about a topic will bleed into your writings, and your readers will be able to feel it too.

That's why I really want you to think about the topic areas that interest you most and focus on those. Are you someone who is fascinated by tech? Then you may want to create content in that field. Or maybe sports are more your thing? There are plenty of good sporting companies that could use a professional writer.

If you're not totally sure what interests you enough to want to spend your days writing about it, think about the things that make you so passionate that, when you speak about them, you could talk for hours and hours on end. Consider also your education, work experiences, hobbies, life experiences, and anything else that you've been through that would make you an expert in that field.

Now, if you're like me when I first started out, you just read the word 'expert' and felt a little tightening in your tummy. You may have even started to sweat a little because now you're thinking that you're not qualified to be an expert in the topic area you've chosen.

That's why it's important that we stop right now and help you understand exactly what an expert is. An expert is not just someone with a PhD or some other advanced degree after their name. It's also not just someone who knows almost all there is to know about a particular topic.

An expert is simply someone who knows more about a particular topic than the average person. Read that again. An expert is someone who simply knows more about a particular topic than the average person. Let's look at a couple of examples.

If you have a Chinese pug and know more about that particular breed than the average person, you are an expert on pugs and someone who others can learn from. This puts you in a good position to work with pug breeders who need content for their website or other marketing materials.

Maybe, like me, you spend a lot of time reading and researching topics related to natural health because you really enjoy the idea of taking care of your own body without subjecting it to harsh chemicals or other substances. That makes you an expert in this field.

Still stumped? Think about the things your family, friends, or co-workers come to you for when they want information. These are likely areas that you have some expertise in and would be a natural to write about.

Your Writing Style

Another consideration when identifying your niche is your writing style. For instance, I'm a conversational writer, which basically means that I write like I talk. I know this because, whenever a family member or friend reads what I've written, whether on my blog or in one of my online articles, they always say, "When I read that piece, I could so hear you saying it!"

This type of writing style has gotten me a lot of gigs, primarily because a lot of readers prefer to take in content that is easy to understand and doesn't use a lot of big, academic words. It's also helped me as a ghostwriter because, after talking to a client briefly, I can usually write like they speak, which means that their blogs sound like they wrote them themselves.

While this works for my clients, this type of writing isn't accepted for detailed medical journals, technical writings (like contracts or product instruction pamphlets), or academic papers, so I wouldn't be any good at those types of jobs. Plus, that type of writing is dry to me as I prefer to be able to put some emotion into my content.

But maybe you prefer creating academic or technical pieces over writing conversationally sounding blogs and similar content? If so, then that writing is for you!

Where You'd Like to Be Published

Another way to hone down your niche is to think about where you'd like to be published. Asked another way: What types of newspapers, magazines, trade journals, or online sites would you be absolutely thrilled to see your name on as a byline to an article?

When I first started out, I had a goal to be published by *Cosmopolitan*. I don't really know why I targeted that magazine specifically (other than that I liked reading the small stories their readers sent in; I think they were listed under "confessions" or something like that), but I felt that, if I could just get published there, that would tell me that I'd finally made it to the big league.

I'd love to tell you that I achieved that goal, but I didn't. I did reach out once or twice, but never heard back. Honestly, looking back now, I'm okay with that outcome because I'm not real fond of the direction *Cosmo* has decided to take, which means that I wouldn't feel proud to have it listed in my portfolio.

Instead, I've had my articles picked up by other publications that are just as well-known—like *Country Living*, *Woman's Day*, and *Costco Connection*—but that I'm also more than comfortable sharing with potential clients who want to know where they can find my work.

So, think about which publications you'd like to see *your* name published with. That may give you some idea of what type of niche you want to target.

Of course, once you know what area you want to work in and what topics you'd enjoy writing about while making a comfortable living doing it, the next step is to learn what it takes to write like a professional writer. This is something I refer to as "learning the craft."

4. Learn the Craft

While some people are naturally good writers, I don't feel that I fall into this category. Granted, writing may be easier for me than for others, but sometimes I really struggle to say what I want to say in a way that is both informational and fun to read.

At first, I really wasn't sure how to learn the craft without paying a lot of money to do it. Certainly, taking college level classes is one way to learn how to become a better writer. However, if you're like I am, I prefer to take less traditional (and cheaper) routes.

Plus, when I set my mind to figuring something out, I don't want to be dripped the information over the course of several weeks or months. I want to go through it at my own pace, which is often quite a bit faster than typical courses allow.

Fortunately, there are several places you can go to learn more about writing that don't require taking out a student loan or sitting idly by until someone else tells you that you're ready to proceed. The first is books.

Read Successful Writers' Books

One option that I've thoroughly enjoyed and actually continue to learn a lot from to this day is reading books written by other writers who've already figured out how to be a success in this field.

The one that made the biggest impact on me in my early writing days is Stephen King's *On Writing*. This was completely unexpected to me because, though there's no denying the fact that King has been super successful in his writing career, I've never really been a huge fan. Not that he's not a good writer, because he is. His books are just not the type of genre I'm typically into.

That being said, he did make a lot of great points in this particular book that have stuck with me throughout my writing career and implement quite often still today. The first is the importance of being strong enough to "kill your darlings."

What King is referring to with this statement is the fact that, for writers, our words are essentially our babies. We create them and bring them to live. We love and nurture them and hope that, some day, with the right amount of care, they'll grow up to leave a major mark on this world.

Sadly though, sometimes our babies, our words, don't quite leave the type of impact we want. This is when we have to be strong enough to go through the daunting task of letting them go.

I've run into this several times myself, initially thinking that I've come up with a clever phrase or idea in my writings. To me, whatever I wrote is absolutely brilliant and I'm excited to include it in my work.

Yet, if I'm being totally honest with myself in the editing process, I know that it either doesn't add to my piece or, worse yet, detracts from it. But, oftentimes I've become so married to my words that I want to keep them even if they ultimately bring my piece down. I'm too afraid to let them go.

To help put this idea into context, it would be like me adding a chapter to this book about how to become a health writer. Though I could give you a lot of great information that could help you get started, the reality is that most people reading this won't choose health and wellness as their niche. Therefore, this could really bring the book down.

This same bit of advice about "killing your darlings" also helps when you're working as a freelance writer for others as one of the worst pieces of feedback you can get is that your content is nothing but "fluff" because you didn't cut the irrelevant stuff out. I know. I've gotten this type of response before.

That's why, when creating content for clients, you should aim to provide them work that has already had the unnecessary words removed. The less editing they have to do themselves, the more projects they'll gladly assign you in the future.

King has other great tidbits in *On Writing*, which is why I recommend his book, especially if you're new to the field. Other writers I've learned a lot from include Joe Vitale (*Hypnotic Writing*), Sally Hogshead (*Fascinate*), and Robert Lee Brewster (*Writer's Market*). Each one has contributed to my ability to earn a comfortable living as a freelance writer in one way or another.

Though these are some of my favorites, the key is to find writers that you admire and respect and see if they've created any books or blog posts that share their insight on what it takes to be a good writer.

Read Highly Followed Blogs

Some successful writers make it super easy to get inside their head and learn from them by sharing their knowledge and expertise in their own blogs. The great thing about this option is that you're able to pick and choose the ones most relevant to you and your niche without having to find time in your busy schedule to read an entire book.

Plus, by subscribing to their blogs, you can get their writing-related wisdom delivered effortlessly to your inbox. It really doesn't get easier than that.

I've had a blog on my own website (www.ChristinaMDeBusk.com) for years. Though I've varied on how often I contribute to it, my subscriber list continues to grow, which tells me that people like reading blogs as a way to learn the craft.

Other blogs to consider checking out are those written by successful bloggers who specialize in writing for a living. According to the RSS Reader Feedspot[v], as of the publication of this book, these include:

- Goins, Writer – *goinswriter.com/blog*
- The Write Practice – *thewritepractice.com*
- Helping Writers Become Authors – *kmweiland.com*
- Live Write Thrive – *livewritethrive.com*
- Make a Living Writing – *makealivingwriting.com*
- Write to Done – *writetodone.com*
- The Creative Penn – *thecreativepenn.com*
- Writers In The Storm – *writersinthestormblog.com*
- Writer Unboxed – *writerunboxed.com*
- Writers Write – *writerswrite.co.za*

Any one of these can give you more direction as to how to hone your craft as each one shares what has worked for them when it comes to their writing careers.

If you like reading blogs in other areas, pay attention to how they're structured, their length, and how the author writes. Look for themes across some of your favorite online content sites and incorporate them into *your* writings for the same type of effects. By mirroring people who've already mastered that type of writing, you're setting yourself up for greater success.

Now that I've said that, I also feel compelled to tell you that, though it's good to emulate the pros, it's still important to keep your own voice when creating content that is going to be published in your name. The more you try to 100 percent copy someone else, the more you'll get lost in the shuffle and the less you'll stand out.

Think about the writers you like to read. You're drawn to them for their unique style, for the way they write. It's the same with music. It's the individual quirkiness or style of the musicians you prefer that keeps you coming back to their songs time and time again.

That's why, when working on your own stuff, you want to focus on providing content that, when someone else reads it, they'll be able to instantly tell that you were the one who wrote it. It'll benefit you in the long run if your goal is to make a name for yourself.

Take an Online Workshop

When most people hear that I'm a freelance writer who has published my own books, their first response is generally something along the lines of, "Wow! I've always wanted to write a book myself!" After hearing this more times than I can count, I decided that I could really help others by walking them through the book writing and publishing process.

This first started with offering in-person workshops at my local library. The response was amazing and I was excited about how many people took the time out of their busy lives to attend. Then, when talking with some of them prior to or immediately after the workshop, I learned that they also wanted an online option …a course they could take from the comfort of their own home.

That drove me to create an online book-writing workshop on a platform called Thinkific. (Here's the link if you want to see what I'm talking about: http://become-an-author-writer.thinkific.com/collections.)

People who take this course learn the same 10 steps that I share in my in-person workshop, yet they can do it on their own time and at their own pace. Plus, when they choose that option, they still get the personal experience of working with me because I include a free 30-minute coaching session for each student.

Once that was up, I started thinking about all of the people who've expressed interest in writing for a living. Shouldn't they have a workshop too?

That's my next step, and one I intend to take the moment this book is published. If I'm successful, it's probably already up and running at the link above!

Of course, I'm not the only writer offering this type of learning option, so you definitely have your choice of workshops in this area, enabling you to choose the one best suited to you.

The only other online writing courses that I have some experience with are the ones through Make a Living Writing (makealivingwriting.com). Though they're not all courses in the traditional sense of the word, I found their informational downloads helpful when growing my writing career.

For a short time, I even joined one of their mastermind groups. To be fair, I did learn a lot during my time with them, but I cancelled my membership a short while later as I also felt like the group was too money focused for me. I'm all for earning more cash, but since that isn't really what motivates me, I actually found that I become more uninspired than inspired, which told me that it was time to move on.

Hire a Writing Coach

Hiring a coach to help you learn the tricks of the trade and reach your writing goals can provide many benefits. One of the most notable is that you get to learn from their experiences without having to make the same mistakes yourself. This can save you a ton of time, and even more frustration.

A writing coach is also someone to bounce ideas off of. Someone who already works in the field and has a pretty good idea of what does and does not work.

Plus, with the internet, you don't even have to be in the same geographic area of the coach you select. All you need is a good connection and decent bandwidth and you can use any number of video or audio platforms for your regularly scheduled sessions.

Admittedly, this option can be somewhat costly, especially if you're just starting out and don't have much of a budget. However, sometimes making an initial investment is enough to catapult you to a higher level of income at a much faster rate, making it more than worth it when all is said and done.

Although I don't write or read young adult literature, for some reason, a lot of writers in this niche have reached out to me over the years, asking me for input and advice about how to get their writing careers off the ground. I've actually found that I enjoy helping this demographic, but it also gave me an idea about how to expand on my current business and provide even more services. I could become a writing coach!

I'm almost ashamed to admit that I hadn't thought about this option before, but, what can I say. I was busy writing! But now, when I thought about all of the ways I could help up-and-coming writers achieve higher levels of success with less stress, coaching only makes sense.

When picking a coach for you, you likely want someone who has experience in your niche area. Every type of writing is different, so the more they know about the one you want to work in, the better this person will be able to help you.

For instance, if someone is interested in writing in the health and wellness niche or in personal development, I would be a good choice because those are the areas I work in most. However, if someone wants to write for tech companies, I would *not* be a good coach for them. I've never worked in that industry, therefore, I don't necessarily know what it takes to succeed as that type of writer.

It's also important to remember that not every coach will be a good match for you and your personality. I've had some clients come to me for coaching and, in the first session, I realized that we're not going to work well together because we're just too different.

In fact, that's pretty much why I offer my first coaching session free. I think it's only fair to research this up front, before taking any money, only to later realize that I can't give them the type of coaching relationship they deserve.

A lot of coaches do this, offering a complimentary session, which makes finding a good match a little easier. And if you talk to one and don't quite feel a connection, talk to another. Keep searching until you find the person who you feel most comfortable with and can help you reach your writing goals.

As you're learning more about how to become the freelance writer you want to be, you also want to start thinking about your brand, which is the subject of our next chapter.

5. Develop Your Brand

As a freelance writer, you are, by and large your own brand. What is brand?

Business Dictionary defines brand as a "unique design, sign, symbol, words, or a combination of these, employed in creating an image that identifies a product and differentiates it from its competitors. Over time, this image becomes associated with a level of credibility, quality, and satisfaction in the consumer's mind.[vi]"

Sounds complex, right? Well, a brand is basically something that, when someone sees something that you put out, they instantly think of you and your business.

For instance, if you're driving down the road and you see big yellow arches, you immediately know that it's a McDonalds. If you see the swoosh, you think of Nike.

The earlier you establish *your* brand—your own personal design, sign, symbol, words, or any combination of these—the easier it will be for others to recognize your work. And the more comfortable they'll become with you.

This last part is critical as the three keys to effective marketing are to get your target market to: 1) like, 2) know, and 3) trust you. The more you're able to reinforce these qualities, the stronger your relationship with your clients and readers.

How to Create a Brand

One way to create a brand is to come up with a logo for your business. Here's mine:

Of course, this is pretty simple and basic, but when my clients see it, they think of me. When creating your own icon or logo, you can be creative as you'd like.

You can also spend as little or as much as you'd like. Some logo designers charge hundreds for helping you come up with just the right images and fonts, or you can do like me and create your own design cost-free. There are also some websites that can help for less than $100.

Additionally, the color scheme on all of my marketing materials matches my logo to further enhance my brand. I use various shades of green primarily because green is associated with health and wellness and that's where I do a majority of my work.

Think of these things when creating your own brand and you can come up with a logo that accurately represents you while also appealing to your target market. Just keep in mind that you want a brand that you can apply across all of your marketing platforms, starting with your website.

Setting up a Website

Just last week I met a woman who used to write for the *L.A. Times* and, somehow, we got on the subject of websites. When I told her I had one, she looked at me all wide-eyed and started talking about how she couldn't afford a website.

That was a little confusing to me because there are so many free website platforms. There's WordPress, Wix, Weebly, Yola, and countless others. Really, you have your choice of any number of options for getting your business online, even if you don't have a big starting budget.

I mentioned this to hear and that's when she revealed that she didn't realize that. Instead, she relied on information provided by someone she'd once spoken to who told her that it takes thousands of dollars to set up a website. They were wrong.

Now, I'll be the first to admit that having a website professionally done is always preferred if you can afford it. For a number of reasons.

One, having someone else design your website keeps you from wasting valuable writing time (which is time you could be earning money) trying to figure it out yourself. Unless you're a wiz with tech and graphics, by the time you learn the ins and outs of setting up an effective website that not only attracts potential clients, but keeps them coming back for more, you probably could have completed a number of paying jobs.

Two, sites designed by pros typically look more professional and appealing to the eye. This is critical because you only have one opportunity to make a first impression, and you want that impression to be a good one.

That being said, I'm also a budget girl, so I opted to take the cheaper route and create my own website using Wix. (My domain is www.christinamdebusk.com if you want to check it out). Overall, I've been more than happy with their setup and find it pretty easy to use, even though I'm not always the most creative when it comes to graphics.

I do opt for a premium site though, which means that, instead of having a totally free site, I do pay about $150 a year, which is less than $13 per month. To me, this expense is worth it, mainly because the premium account enables me to remove the word "Wix" from my URL, making my site look more professional.

I also chose this option because I always have quick and easy control over my website and don't have to rely on someone else to make updates as I want them. I change my content often enough where, to me, it would be a pain to turn this type of control over.

What pages should you have on your website? There are a number of options, but I currently have six. They are:

1. *Home page*, which lists my services, areas of specialty, education and experience.

2. *Testimonials page*, which contains input from past and current clients, sharing how they've enjoyed working with me and what makes me different (better) than my competitors.

3. *A store page*, which is where visitors can find all of my books, workshops, and any other products I've created. (For the time being, I've also added some of the books that are currently on my bookshelf, with links to them on Amazon. I do this 1) because a lot of people ask for recommendations and, 2) for affiliate marketing purposes, which means I earn a commission on any sales that occur by someone clicking the link and then buying the book.)

4. *About page,* which shares a little bit of my story and who I am personally.

5. *Blog,* where you'll find my thoughts and input on writing or one of the areas I specialize in.

6. *Contact page,* where people can fill out a form with their name, email address, and a brief description of the services they want so I can get back with them.

If you're just starting out and don't have any testimonials or anything to sell in a store, that's okay. At least set up a home page and contact page. You can add the rest as you go.

This gives you a website URL you can share with anyone you speak to who is interested in your services. I also include a link to it in all of my bios on other sites (like my bio on *Chiropractic Economics* or *Businessing Magazine*), so readers who enjoy my work can click back to my site.

I put in my signature line on my outgoing emails as well. By listing it in all of these different places, this continuously reminds my clients and prospective clients to go to my site for the most updated information about my products and services.

Social Media Considerations

If you go to my site, you'll notice that I've also included links so my visitors can easily connect with me on social media. Again, the more places I can connect with my target audience, the more likely it is they'll think of me when they need the products and services I offer.

To be completely honest though, social media is the one area I love to hate. I love it because it makes it possible to connect with people you wouldn't normally be able to connect with, such as those who live on opposite sides of the world. However, I also hate it in that sometimes it can be confusing and there are so many options to consider. For instance, should I use Facebook? What about Twitter? Hmm…maybe Instagram? It's so overwhelming!

What I've found to work the best, especially when just starting out, is to focus mainly on the sites that 1) you know the most about and 2) that most of your clients and potential customers are on. According to a poll I recently did of my followers, these are primarily Facebook and Twitter for me. I'm also on LinkedIn.

Facebook is good for promoting new products, like when you release a new book or create an online workshop. Twitter seems to work best for sharing published content, which is basically any content that is credited to you. LinkedIn has been a great way to connect with professionals who could use my services.

If you plan to use more than one social media site to promote your business, you may find great value in signing up for services (like Hootsuite or Sprout Social) that will post on all of your social media sites at a prescheduled date and time. I do my own posting based on whatever I'm feeling on a specific day, so this option wouldn't work well for me. But if you'd rather set up your posts a week or two at a time, this is something to consider. It's all about finding what works best for you.

When setting up your social media accounts, remember to stick to your brand. This means that each one should have the same general look so, when your customer searches for it or sees it, they instantly know it's you.

I also highly recommend that you create separate social media profiles for your business than the ones you use personally. This enables you to share private pictures, thoughts, and events with family and friends without worrying about who else will see it.

Business Cards

I also recommend that you get business cards to help promote yourself as a writer. I can't tell you how many times I've met people while out and about and, when they find out that I write for a living, they ask for my card. In fact, I gave out three today alone!

You don't have to spend a fortune on them either. As long as they have your name, "Freelance Writer" or some variation of this, your email address, website URL, and telephone number, you're good. I just ordered a new batch yesterday from Vistaprint and I think I paid $15 for 100 of them. Order more and you get a better deal.

Don't forget about your brand when creating these either because, again, you want the person who gets your card to start to get to know you. When they go to your website and find the same general feel, both in color and design, you start to strengthen that relationship and draw them in.

Okay. So you've got your supplies, you've identified your writing niche, you're learning more about the craft of writing every day, and have established your brand with at least a website and business cards. At this point, it's time to start finding clients.

6. How to Find Clients

You can be the best writer in the world, but if you don't develop a solid client base, your living isn't going to be anywhere near comfortable. This starts with finding your very first client.

And though many new freelance writers like to believe the old adage, "If you build it, they will come" (I've been guilty of this!), they learn soon enough how untrue this statement is. In fact, your clients aren't going to come to you at all, at least not until you've established a solid reputation for yourself. No, you must go to them.

It's also important to realize that not all clients are created equal. In other words, you not only want to find clients, but you want to find the best clients you can.

Defining "Best"

As I mentioned previously, when I first started out, I would take any job that paid. Even if it was just a little bit of money, I figured it was okay because it got me experience. But it also got me something else. Burnt out.

A majority of the problem revolved around most of the clients being one-off. This means that they only wanted one piece of content and then our working relationship would be done.

The problem with this approach is that sometimes it takes a lot of back-and-forth to determine exactly what a new client wants as far as style, information, and tone. That's time that went unpaid, not to mention the fact that it can be frustrating to put that much effort into figuring out the ins and outs of someone who only wants you to write for them once.

That's why now I typically only work for clients who want more than just one piece of content (unless it's a bigger project that is going to make it worth my time). I want long-term relationships that enable me to write more efficiently over time because I become familiar with the client and what he or she wants.

I also strive to work with businesses and business owners who already understand the value of good content. That way I'm not spending a bunch of time trying to educate them about how important their content is or justifying my not-always-the-lowest price.

Though it may be hard to stick to these sorts of qualifications in the beginning, both are something I would strive for as you become a more experienced and established writer. Your sanity will thank you.

Publications vs Businesses

Paying clients generally come in one of two forms: publications or businesses. For instance, I write for two publications—*Chiropractic Economics* and *MASSAGE Magazine*—every month, but I also have individual entrepreneurs and business owners who I provide content to regularly as well, like a motivational speaker who I help with weekly blogs and a couple of marketing firms that need multiple articles ghostwritten for their clients.

The one major difference between the two is, if you write for publications, typically they'll give you your own byline. This means that you're credited with writing the piece because your name is attached to it as the author. This can help you build your portfolio, giving other potential clients the opportunity to see your writing style and tone.

Writing for businesses on the other hand typically involves no one but you and the business owner or representative knowing that you are the one who created the content. In these instances, I often have to sign a non-disclosure, which means that I can't share that work as part of my portfolio.

Neither one is good or bad, right or wrong, they're just different in that regard. You can choose to go for projects that involve one over the other, or you can do like me and do both.

When it comes to writing for publications, most have their submission guidelines right on their website. If you have a hard time finding this information, just do an internet search for "submission guidelines for (publication name)" and it should take you to the page.

I've also done LinkedIn searches to see if I could identify who the editors were for the publications I want to write for. Though some choose to not answer an inMail from someone they don't know, others have been kind enough to provide a response.

In fact, reaching out to an editor on LinkedIn was how I wound up getting published by *Woman's Day* and *Country Living*. I figured out who the person responsible for my type of content was, pitched an idea, she accepted, and I wrote it up.

If you decide to take this route, you want to give the editor a potential title for your story, share why it would be important to their readers, and provide the basic information you intend to write about. If you plan to interview someone for the piece, it helps to share that up front as well.

Some publications pay their writers and some don't. Though I prefer to write for sites that pay, for obvious reasons, there is some value in writing for ones that don't.

For instance, I have pieces on Everyday Power Blog and The Possibility of Change Blog, two of the most visited personal development blogs on the web. And, though I wasn't paid for them, my byline links their readers back to my website, boosting my traffic in that way.

I can also use those pieces in my portfolio, which is huge when you're just starting out. Not to mention, the more blogs I can get my content on, the easier it is to establish myself as an expert in my field.

Reaching out to business owners takes a completely different approach, one that took me a long time to learn. Yet, through a lengthy trial and error process, I've finally perfected my cold-call emails to the point where I'm able to get about a 10 percent response.

It may not seem like much, but this is pretty good considering that the average response is less than 1 percent[vii]. This means that, while the average freelance writer like me gets 1 response out of every 100 emails that are sent out, I get closer to 10. Yay for me!

What wound up working the best was a short, concise email asking if there was anything I could help my prospect with content-wise. My goal was to let them know that I was there to make their life easier, not to ask for their money.

In addition, I made the email personable and, whenever possible, included some information that showed them that I took the time to check them out first. I wasn't just contacting anyone and everyone, hoping to get a bite.

For example, when I reach out to speakers to see if they want help writing books they can sell at their gigs, I mention one of the blog posts or something personal they've shared on their website. I've had a number of positive responses about how much they appreciated me taking the time to learn a little bit about them before asking them to work with me.

If you decide to take this route, remember to be yourself, but keep the email concise. Also, don't try to sell yourself. Instead, focus on *their* needs and see what you can do to help *them* with whatever they may find a struggle. Your email should be all about them versus all about you.

As far as which businesses to target, that depends on what type of writing you choose to go into. As a health and wellness writer focused on natural treatments and prevention, I've reached out to wellness centers, dentists, chiropractors, and fitness facilities. Because I also offer content in personal development, I've cold-emailed life coaches, psychologists, and mental health professionals.

If your goal is to be a tech writer, you'll likely want to reach out to tech companies or tech publications. If you want to focus on writing resumes, then you may find work with colleges, job placement centers, or any other place where you're likely to find a large group of people looking to enter the workforce.

To recap, first you want to consider the type of writing you want to get into and what type of clients it could benefit the most. From there, your next step is to figure out who you should reach out to at that publication or business, then reach out to let them know that you're there to help.

This isn't always easy to do though as how you reach out can greatly affect your response.

Tips for Reaching Out

Personally, I choose email as my method for reaching out because then people can read it at a time that is most convenient for them. This means that I'm not interrupting them when they're in the middle of something big, potentially decreasing the odds that they'll be willing to listen to my services.

I've also found that I get the best response when I reach out mid-week, on Tuesdays, Wednesdays, or Thursdays. Mondays are often a bit hectic for most people, making it easier to just delete my electronic inquiry versus having to consider the addition of one more project being added to their already overflowing plate. Fridays have also elicited minimal responses, likely because people are looking forward to the weekend and a few days off, so the last thing they want to do is think about starting a new project.

During slower times, I'll send out 20-25 cold emails every day on those middle three days of the week. Sometimes I got a response immediately. Other times, it takes the person a couple of weeks to think about it get back with me. Either way, I always tell them that I appreciate their response, even if it's a "no."

Remember that your only goal in this initial contact is to 1) plant the seed for the services you offer, and 2) to see if they're open to a conversation. No selling.

In fact, I don't ask potential clients for work at all at this stage. I simply pose the question about whether or not they've thought about writing a book or a keeping a blog. And, if so, I ask whether they'd find value in talking about their options with an experienced writer.

I'm not trying to make a sale here. I only want to open the door and get them thinking about what type of help I could possibly provide.

I think part of what makes my email campaigns so successful is also that they're not about me at all. Instead, they're about my prospective clients and what I can do to make *their* lives easier. Who doesn't want that?

What About Writing Platforms?

One of the most controversial discussions in all of my writing groups is whether you should offer your services on a writing platform. Unfortunately, this isn't an easy one for me because I have somewhat mixed feelings.

When I first started out, I got a majority of my jobs on Elance, which is now Upwork. The thing I enjoyed most about this platform was that I got to pick the jobs that interested me most, enter a bid on them, and a lot of times I got the work.

In fact, I got so much work and such positive reviews from my clients on Elance, that I soon found myself in the top one percent of their writers. And there were more than 250,000 in total, so that's pretty good!

I also did a little work on other platforms too, but when I actually sat down and figured out how much I was making, a lot of times, it didn't even come out to minimum wage. No wonder I was feeling burnt out! I was working my tail off and barely getting paid.

I'll always be thankful for these platforms though because, in doing the thousands of jobs that I did on them, I was able to really learn how to write while at least earning something. It wasn't much, but it helped pay my bills.

That being said, now that I have some experience in the field, I stay away from them completely. One, I now charge more than most other writers on those sites, which means that, even though my work may be higher quality, the person hiring writers likely won't want to pay for it when they're getting lower bids.

Also, as we just discussed, most of the projects on these platforms are one-off projects and I don't want to spend a lot of time learning how to write for someone only to have them ask for just one piece of content. I'd rather work for a business or publication who needs continual content, providing me with a more stable income.

I guess that if you sum it up, my general feeling is that writing platforms are a great way to get experience, but your goal shouldn't necessarily be to stay on them forever. Get your experience, build your portfolio, then go after clients who are willing to pay for higher quality work.

Speaking of clients who are willing to pay higher prices, you may be wondering just how much you should charge. I know this was an amazingly difficult decision for me, so I've dedicated the whole next chapter to it in the hopes that it isn't quite so difficult for you.

7. Setting Your Rates & Fees

When setting your rates and fees, you want to charge enough to make the work worth your time, but you also want to be competitive and not set your prices so high that no one wants to hire you. How do you find the middle ground?

On the bright side, sometimes rates aren't an issue because certain publications and businesses have preset amounts that they pay all of their writers. In effect, they pay what they pay and you either accept it or you don't write for them.

I remember when I came across this for the first time. Starting out on writing platforms, I had always named my own prices. Yet, once I began actually reaching out to clients and publications who had long-standing relationships with writers, I was now being told the payment amount. I almost felt relieved.

No more trying to come up with a price that they would hopefully accept, biting my nails until I heard back from them and constantly second-guessing whether I charged too much or, just as bad, not enough. Talk about stress!

But if you're reaching out to entrepreneurs or companies that don't have these preset rates, you're likely going to have to take the lead and tell them how much you charge. What's the right amount?

Education and Experience

One of the first considerations when setting your rates is how much education you have in writing. Do you have a degree in journalism or English literature, for instance? If so, you might be able to charge more than someone who does not.

Because my degree was in sociology, psychology, social work, and criminal justice, I had no formal writing education that I could use to leverage higher pay. That's primarily why I charged so little when I got started. I didn't feel like I had the right to request more.

Now, that doesn't mean that you have to do the same. If you're naturally a good writer, then you may be able to start higher up on the scale. But, if like me, you're a little unsure of your abilities, you may decide to do what I did and keep your rates lower until you have enough experience to charge more, which is the second consideration.

Maybe you've spent the last 10 years as a career coach, which involved helping people write killer resumes. That would enable to charge you more on projects relating to these types of writing.

Whatever your education and experience, remember that the cool thing about working for yourself is that you have the ability to adjust your prices any time you want. So, if you set them at a certain amount and don't get any clients, you can always lower your rates a little and see if that makes a difference. Another option would be to keep them right where they are, but learn more skills or take on a new writing niche and see if that increases your number of jobs.

If you're not getting any jobs at all or barely enough to survive on, don't just assume that your pricing is the reason. Maybe you're not reaching out as effectively as you could be, or perhaps you're going after the wrong clientele.

In this case, it never hurts to follow a 'no' response with a quick email that asks them if they're willing to briefly share why they chose someone else. Some may not take the time to answer, but for those who do, the information can be invaluable because it helps you better tailor your approach to the next person, increasing your chances of getting a 'yes.'

Alternatively, if you're getting so much work you can't keep up, then it's probably time to raise your prices because you're likely charging too little. Plus, the more in demand you become, the more you can charge, so you should be adjusting your prices regularly anyway.

3 Ways to Set Your Prices

When determining your price, there are three basic ways to do it. The first is to charge your clients an hourly rate. The benefit of this option is that you get paid for all of the time you put into a project.

For example, if you have to do two hours of research before you can even begin to write, then you will get paid for this time. And if they request any edits, you'll be reimbursed for this as well.

Though this is great in theory, I've found that some clients are hesitant with hourly rates because they don't know how much they'll wind up paying in the end. It makes it hard for them to budget because they don't know whether the work will take you one hour or ten.

Plus, some may accuse you of "milking" the project if it takes longer than they expected. For these reasons, should you decide to quote an hourly rate, I would suggest that you give them a basic idea of how long you expect the project to take.

You may even agree to a preset cap where, if you go over a certain number of hours, you don't charge for them. This may give you a competitive edge because you're telling your client that you respect their budget and also that you're not going to take any longer than necessary because, if you do, you're the one who will eat the cost.

I've worked some projects this way, primarily if it's something new and I have no idea how long it will take. I've also used this strategy if the client also wants to have regular meetings or content strategy sessions. Normally though, I set my rates using the second option, which is to give a per-project quote.

After outlining exactly what the client wants, I simply think about how many hours I think it will take me to give it to them, allowing for a little extra time to cover things like phone calls and emails with the client, or anything else that may take up my time (like editing requests or added content). I multiply that number by what I want to make hourly and come up with a price that way.

A number of my clients have thanked me for charging using this method because then they know up front what the project cost will be. Additionally, I don't hurt our working relationship if I can't get through the work as fast as I thought because time is no longer an issue. Not to mention, if I get the project done more quickly than I anticipated, it's almost like earning a bonus.

A third option, and one that I use with clients who want articles only, but in varying lengths, is to charge per word. This is actually a pretty common practice as many companies hire writers to write posts according to word count, so they're able to pay based on the length of content needed for a specific piece.

What amounts specifically do I charge? I'll share that information with you, but I also want to include a disclaimer. My prices are modified all of the time, so the numbers I'm giving you may be very different by the time you read this book.

Currently, if I bid a project based on how long it will take me, I calculate based on $50-$100 per hour. The reason for the range is twofold. First, if I really want the project, whether because I know I'll enjoy it or if I feel it will really help my portfolio, I may go with a lower rate.

The higher rate usually comes into play if I really don't care if I get the work or if I have to do a lot of research because I'm not as familiar with the topic. That way, if I *am* hired, I don't mind as much because I'm being better paid for my time. This is also how I calculate if someone wants to hire me by the hour.

For the per-word pieces, I charge anywhere from $0.10 to $0.25 per word. The lower amount applies if there is limited research necessary, thus taking less of my time. The higher rate applies if I need to do interviews or if a piece is going to take me longer than normal based on client needs.

As far as the amount that *you* charge, regardless of which method you use, you want it to be an amount that makes you excited about the project. In my early writing days, I kept my rates super low just to increase the odds I'd get the job. While this definitely kept me busy, I also started to feel burned out.

Because I was giving my clients such a deal, working for pennies on the dollar, any time they wanted edits or something that would take more time, I started to resent them (even though I set the amount). Over time, I dreaded working with them more and more, which meant that each new assignment I got caused me more stress.

Deciding that enough was enough and knowing that, if I didn't change, my career as a freelance writer wasn't going to last, I decided that it was time to set my rates based on an amount consistent with other professional writers, but was still a good deal for the client.

I know you were probably hoping for a super easy formula or some way to arrive at an exact amount, but setting your rates isn't that easy because your individual education, experience, and desired pay all come into play.

If you're still unsure what rate is best, one option is to research other writers who are already working in the field you want to enter and see what they charge. Then check out their background and see how yours compares.

Writer's Digest is a publication that also provides a fairly detailed spreadsheet, sharing the high, low, and average rates for a bunch of different writing types. It even breaks them down hourly and per word so you can charge based on the method you prefer.

To access its most current chart, just go online and search "writer's digest freelance rates" and it should come up somewhere in the top ten search results. You can also buy the latest *Writer's Market* book as that contains this chart too. Last I checked, it's available in both print and e-book form.

Your pricing model is only half of the income equation because, if you don't get paid, you're not going to be in the freelance writing business for long…no matter what you charge! So, how can you set yourself up in a way that increases the likelihood that you'll actually get paid?

Let's talk about that now.

8. Getting Paid

When setting up your freelance writing business, one of the first things you want to decide is how you'll accept money from your clients. What methods of payment are you going to allow them to use?

Payment Methods

I've worked for entrepreneurs and business owners from all over the world as I've had clients in the United Kingdom, Australia, Israel, and Greece, just to name a few. And that's in addition to the ones in almost every state across the U.S.

PayPal has worked well in these cases because 1) it's available in most geographic locations, and 2) it converts other currencies into U.S. dollars. This makes it convenient for both my clients and I, and allows me to work more easily with individuals and companies not within the U.S.

Like other payment platforms, PayPal does take a certain portion of your earnings though, so you need to realize up front should you choose to allow this method of payment. Currently, their rate is 2.9% of the total amount paid plus $0.30. So, if I charge $150 on a project and the client pays through PayPal, I wind up with $145.35 (150 x .029 + .30 = $4.65 fee; 150 – 4.65 = $145.35).

Of course, I'd rather walk away with the entire amount, but PayPal is trusted and a lot of people use them, so I find the pros outweigh the cons. Plus, I can write the fees off on my taxes at the end of the year, so that helps take the sting out a bit.

For U.S. based clients with whom I have a long-standing relationship or are bigger organizations, I also allow them to directly deposit the payments into my checking account. This option is great because there are no fees taken out and I have immediate access to the money (although, in fairness, PayPal transfers the money within 1-2 days of initiating the request, so it isn't unreasonable; and they just recently started offering a 30 minute transfer for $0.25).

The last payment method I accept is via check. Though I love the fact that, again, there are no fees, this option generally takes the longest from invoice to receipt of my money, so I avoid it if I can. Some businesses I write for only offer this option, so I have no choice if I want to freelance for them.

There are tons of other payment platforms out there, but these are the ones I use most. I've thought about using invoicing software systems like FreshBooks—the freelance invoicing system suggested by my favorite finance expert Dave Ramsey—but since a large number of my regular clients pay direct or have specifically requested PayPal, I've decided not to take that route at this time. If you're just starting out though, FreshBooks may be worth a look. If Dave Ramsey says it's good, then I trust his advice.

Generally speaking, if a client wants to make payment via a certain method, I try to be as accommodating as I can without risking that I won't get paid at all. Sometimes this is a balancing act, but I can honestly say that I've never been outright stiffed. Some writers aren't that lucky though, which is why choosing when to collect your fee is another critical factor to decide up front.

When to Collect

If a project is going to come with a high bill to my client, or if it involves working with an entrepreneur or business that is not a well-known institution or publication, I always request half of the amount up front as a good faith payment.

This increases my comfort level with the company and the project. And if they do try to stiff me when the work is complete, at least I didn't lose the entire amount.

I also request that the remainder be paid within 30 days of delivery. This gives small business owners ample time to come up with the remaining monies owed, spreading their bill out over time so it doesn't impact their budget quite as much.

Notice that I said that I request payment within 30 days of *delivery*. Initially, I didn't request final payment until the project was completed. That is, until I worked with a few clients who got busy and wouldn't get back to finalize the project for months. Meanwhile, I've already done the work and can't submit a final invoice.

Now that is rectified because they know the final half is due within 30 days of the day I return the drafted project to them. My edits are included in the project quote, so whether I do them before I get paid or after is irrelevant because it doesn't change the final price.

My regular clients who are individuals or small business owners typically pay their invoices within a day or two, sometimes within the hour they're submitted. Some take as long as a week. If two weeks go by, I typically send a payment reminder and that usually does the trick.

Sometimes clients have a predetermined pay schedule, especially if they contract with several writers. For instance, one of the publications I write for submits my invoice to their accounting department right when I send it and pay on Fridays, so I can usually expect the money in my mailbox within 2-3 weeks. Another takes a bit longer, which means that it's closer to two months before I get paid.

These are just the ways I operate payments in my business. Feel free to tweak them any way you'd like to better fit your business and clientele, or to choose any other payment option that you're comfortable with.

For me, the most important thing is to know up front when I can expect payment so I can plan my expenses accordingly. This information also guides me to know when to follow up if nothing comes in. That's why it's important to ask all new clients how they pay and, if possible, set your own parameters clearly at the beginning.

Payment Contracts: Yes or No?

I've had a number of new clients ask whether I wanted them to sign a contract and many are surprised when I say no. But here are my thoughts on this: If I'm taking you on as a new client, then I'm already requesting half of the money up front. If you stiff me on the other half, am I going to take the time to file a lawsuit and go after you? It's not likely because most of my projects are $5,000 or less. It's simply not worth my time.

Plus, I always email my payment expectations up front, asking for a written reply before I start the work. That way, if I ever did decide that an unpaid invoice was big enough or important enough to go to court over, I have black and white proof of our agreement, right along with the other person's acknowledgement and approval of the amount.

Sometimes new clients have their own contracts that they require all of their freelancers to sign. I've read each one and never had a problem signing it as most of it is pretty standard language.

Granted, I have a fairly decent grasp on legal mumbo-jumbo after working in the courts for 15 years, so this is good enough for me. But if you are presented with a contract and are ever confused by what it says *at all*, then it's always advisable to seek legal counsel before signing your name. This is definitely one case where you want to know exactly what you're getting yourself into.

And if you do bigger jobs that are usually higher in price, then it may be worth it to go through the contract creation process. An attorney with contract experience can help you create a template that you can adjust based on each individual client and project. That makes this a one-time expense that you can use over and over again by simply changing out the information.

Taxes and Retirement

One other consideration when it comes to payment is, because you work for yourself, no one is taking out your taxes or saving any money for your retirement. This places the burden solely on you to make sure you have enough of your earnings set aside for both.

As a rule, I always deduct 25 percent of whatever I'm paid and set it aside in a savings account that I keep strictly for tax purposes. That way I won't ever find myself in a position where the IRS wants their money and I don't have it to give them.

Again, talk to your accountant and follow his or her advice as far as how much *you* should withhold and how often you need to pay. There are a ton of regulations (about things like paying your taxes quarterly) and you don't want to violate them, putting you at risk of costly penalties or fines.

For retirement, I set aside at least 15 percent (the amount that Dave Ramsey recommends in his book, *The Total Money Makeover*) in an IRA (Individual Retirement Account).

All of these options can be pretty complex and I'm not qualified to give advice on any of them, so if you're interested in learning more about how to properly save for taxes and retirement, talk to your accountant and/or tax adviser. He or she can help you get everything in place so these issues are no longer a worry, guiding you about exactly what amounts you need to set aside for each.

EIN

One last thing to think about when it comes to getting paid is that some clients will ask you to sign a W-9 for tax purposes. If you've ever filled one out, then you know that it requests your Social Security Number (SSN).

If you're uncomfortable providing this information, you can always apply for an Employer Identification Number, or EIN. This enables you to satisfy tax requirements without giving out your SSN, and you can get one within a matter of minutes right on the IRS website at https://www.irs.gov/businesses/small-businesses-self-employed/apply-for-an-employer-identification-number-ein-online.

9. Other Business Considerations

Now that we've talked about how to decide what type of freelance writing you're going to do; the equipment and supplies you'll need to do it; how you need to brand yourself, find clients, and get paid; it's time to talk about a few other business-related considerations you need to make. One is your business type.

Business Type

Though the overall type of your business is freelance writing, when I refer to business type in this sense, I'm actually talking about how you're going to be legally structured. Specifically, are you going to be a sole proprietor, or will you create an LLC or corporation?

Before I begin, let me preface this section by saying that I am by no means an expert in this area. This means that, ultimately, the option you choose for yourself should be a decision you make with the help of someone like a business attorney or even your accountant. Okay. Now that that's out, let's give you the basics.

I chose to set up my business as a sole proprietor, which means that I own the business by myself, and I and my business are one in the same. One benefit of this type is that it's super simple to set up because there's nothing you really need to do. You simply start to work.

This option does have its disadvantages though. For instance, if someone wanted to sue me, my personal assets are at risk since there's no distinction between me and my business. Plus, if I ever grew my business to the point where someone could potentially want to buy it, it's likely worthless without me in the equation.

A second option is to operate your business under an LLC, which stands for Limited Liability Corporation. One huge plus of taking this route is that your personal and business assets are separate so, if you have an unhappy customer that wants to take you to court, you don't risk losing any of the property you have worked so hard to obtain. However, you do have to take some extra steps legally to get your business registered as an LLC, and your taxes become a little more complicated too.

The last business type is one that I don't know any freelance writers who use and that is creating a corporation. I suppose that if you wound up growing to the point where you hired a bunch of freelance writers under you or you expanded your services to include publishing or some other options, then this one may make more sense. Like LLCs, corporations are more time consuming and require more work to set up, but they also provide some protection of your personal assets.

Record Keeping

Another thing you'll want to decide before opening up shop is what type of record-keeping system you're going to use. This is important for keeping your projects straight (which translates into no missed deadlines), getting paid on time, and for compiling your data for tax filing purposes.

I'm a little ashamed to admit it, but I'm actually pretty old-school in this regard in that I do almost all of my record keeping by hand. I blame it on the fact that I'm infatuated with legal pads and pencils. However, truth be told, it's probably also partly because I'm more than a little apprehensive about learning about and trusting in technology.

I know, I know. I'm sure my fears are unfounded, but it sends me into a mini panic attack when I consider that I could potentially lose my entire record-keeping system if a company's server, software, or app goes down. Plus, the information is always at my fingertips the way I do it, no internet or computer required, which I really like when I'm travelling.

That being said, I don't object to the use of software programs to help you keep better records. I know many professionals who use them and they've been more than happy. It just means that I can't offer an educated opinion on individual options that I could potentially recommend.

But what I *can* tell you is this: whatever system you choose, make sure it makes your life easier instead of harder. If you find a system cumbersome or dread using it, you're increasing the odds that you won't and, before you know it, you'll have a big mess on your hands.

When it comes to your revenue specifically, be sure to select or create a system that will tell you:

- When you sent an invoice
- The amount of the invoice
- Who you sent it to
- When it's overdue

I also keep track of whether or not a fee was deducted from the amount. This makes it easier at tax time to calculate this particular deduction.

I even note in my system how much needs to be set aside for taxes, how much needs to go to retirement, and how much is left over to put toward my business or my pay. Having these figures right in front of me helps me get a more solid picture of my finances whenever I want to know how I'm doing or where I stand.

Part of good record-keeping also means keeping track of your projects so none of them fall through the tracks. If this happens, you start to miss deadlines and, ultimately risk losing clients.

I'm sure it will come as no surprise based on my old-school ways, but I use a small weekly calendar for this purpose. I always have it open on my desk where I can see my week at a glance. I can also easily take it with me when I'm working away from home.

Of course, there are many different electronic schedule-based options available; you may already be using one.

Again, it doesn't matter so much what type of calendar you choose for your freelance writing business, as long as you choose one that you like and will stick with it.

The only type of record-keeping that I actually use my computer for is the Excel spreadsheet I keep for tax purposes. I have columns for all of my earnings based on how they're paid (direct, PayPal, etc.) and I also have columns for any expenses associated with running my business (PayPal fees, office supplies, marketing costs, and things like that).

Again, I cannot stress enough that, although I know a decent amount about these topic areas, I *always, always* suggest that you talk with your tax preparer when setting up your business. Let him or her guide you so you can make the best decision for you.

This person can also tell you what types of deductions you can take, how they want you to keep track of them, and any other information you should tally up when running your freelance writing business. This sets you up for success, while also keeping you as free from legal issues as possible.

Marketing

Regardless of how many times I'd been warned that the phrase "build it and they will come" is a bunch of bull, when I first started out, a small part of me still believed that all I'd have to do to become a sought-after freelance writer is create a website. I had convinced myself that it was only a matter of time before clients would find me and all of these job proposals would be filling my inbox, solely because I was online.

Yeah. Not at all. My email inbox was just as empty the day after my website went live as it was the day before.

Being a freelance writer is no different than owning a shoe store, carpet cleaning business, restaurant, or any other company. If you don't continuously market yourself and your services, no one is going to know you exist.

Sure, maybe once you've been in business for a long time and have a lot of repeat and referral clients, you can relax a little in this area. But only a little, and, until then, you're going to have to work really hard to make yourself known.

Having a website is definitely a good start though, especially if it's search engine optimized (SEO) so your clients can find you easier. Reaching out to individuals and publications you want to work with enables you to get your name out there too.

You can also get a lot of free marketing nowadays thanks to the internet. For instance, you can write a bylined article for a non-paying website and put a link back to your web page in your bio. You can also post about your services on your social media, encouraging your followers to share them with their family and friends.

Depending on what type of writing you decide to get into, it may benefit you to take out an ad in a trade magazine that your target client would likely read. This option will likely cost a couple hundred dollars, but if you get just one client from that post, you can typically get your original investment back, maybe even more if they give you continued work.

Another option is to donate to your favorite charity in your business' name. People like to support business owners who care about people and the community. Plus, you get to feel good while growing your business at the same time.

If you don't have a lot of money to spend on sponsoring or donating to a charitable event, you can at least donate your time or skills. Offer some free web content or content for their fundraising brochures. They'll likely at least give you a mention, which increases awareness that you exist.

Personally, I've found that the best form of marketing ever is word of mouth. That's why I am extremely gracious when my current clients refer their colleagues to me.

I always take the time to send them a thank-you email any time someone contacts me and gives me their name. In fact, I've gotten a lot of jobs over the years this way, and, oftentimes, they've been some of my best clients ever.

Measure Your Results

The final piece of advice I have when it comes to setting up your freelance writing business is to always know your numbers so you can measure your results.

If you've ever watched the show *Shark Tank*, then you know what I'm talking about. If not, suffice it to say that you always want to know what is and what *isn't* working in your business, and you can't know either if you're not keeping track.

While revenues are a great way to judge whether or not you're doing well, other metrics need to be measured as well. For example, I keep track of the cold-call emails I send out to prospective clients, noting how many positive responses I receive, how many emails are returned because of bad addresses, and how many say thanks, but no thanks.

This tells me whether or not I'm wasting my time when reaching out to a certain demographic, or if I'm even picking up enough business to justify the time it takes to filter through each one. I go so far as to note which days of the week I send the emails and what time of day so I can clearly see if I get better results at different times.

Keeping track can help you see where you're the most effective with your marketing, and where you're wasting your time. This is critical when you're in business for yourself because your success or failure depends solely on your ability to make the best of the time you have.

Now Write

Now that you have the basics necessary to set up your freelance writing business, it's time to start taking action.

If you need any help along the way, please don't hesitate to reach out. You can email me at cdebusk13@gmail.com and I'll gladly answer your questions or provide some guidance.

And if you feel like you need a lot of help, I even offer one-on-one coaching where we can spend individualized time together (on video or via phone) to help you make sure you're on the right path.

You can find information about that and all of my other services at www.ChristinaMDeBusk.com.

I'm also planning to create a workshop on becoming a freelance writer, which may even be out by the time you read this book. It will be at this link: http://become-an-author-writer.thinkific.com/collections, so check it out!

In the meantime, get out there and be the freelance writer you want to be. I've got your back and will be pulling for you every step of the way!

You've got this!

References

[i] Occupational Outlook Handbook: Writers and Authors. Bureau of Labor Statistics. https://www.bls.gov/ooh/media-and-communication/writers-and-authors.htm#tab-1

[ii] Freelance Writer Salary. PayScale. http://www.payscale.com/research/US/Job=Freelance_Writer/Hourly_Rate

[iii] Freelance Writer Salaries. Glassdoor. https://www.glassdoor.com/Salaries/freelance-writer-salary-SRCH_KO0,16.htm

[iv] North Branch, MI. City-Data.com. http://www.city-data.com/city/North-Branch-Michigan.html#b

[v] "Top 100 Writing Blogs for Authors and Book Writers." (September 25, 2017). Feedspot. http://blog.feedspot.com/top-100-writing-blogs/

[vi] "Brand." Business Dictionary. http://www.businessdictionary.com/definition/brand.html

[vii] "Average Response Rate to Cold Email." LeadFuze. https://www.leadfuze.com/average-response-rate-to-cold-email/

www.ingramcontent.com/pod-product-compliance
Lightning Source LLC
Chambersburg PA
CBHW070304230526
45470CB00002B/710